Mini Desserts

Mini Desserts

This edition published in 2012

LOVE FOOD is an imprint of Parragon Books Ltd

Parragon
Chartist House
15–17 Trim Street
Bath BA1 1HA, UK

ISBN: 978-1-78186-378-7

Printed in China

Created and produced by Pene Parker and Becca Spry
Author and home economist: Sara Lewis
Photographer: William Shaw

Notes for the reader

This book uses both metric and imperial measurements. Follow the same units of measurements throughout; do not mix metric and imperial. All spoon measurements are level: teaspoons are assumed to be 5 ml, and tablespoons are assumed to be 15 ml. Unless otherwise stated, milk is assumed to be full fat, and eggs and individual fruits are medium.

The times given are an approximate guide only. Preparation times differ according to the techniques used by different people and the cooking times may also vary from those given. Optional ingredients, variations or serving suggestions have not been included in the calculations.

Recipes using raw or very lightly cooked eggs should be avoided by infants, the elderly, pregnant women, convalescents, and anyone suffering from an illness. Pregnant and breastfeeding women are advised to avoid eating peanuts and peanut products. Sufferers from nut allergies should be aware that some of the ready-made ingredients used in the recipes in this book may contain nuts. Always check the packaging before use.

Contents

Introduction

Impress your friends at your next dinner party, birthday celebration or other special occasion with these dainty mini desserts. If you want the option of serving a tiny sweet treat or, for a smart restaurant feel, two or three different desserts on one plate per person, instead of a whole pudding, then these recipes are for you. For an informal gathering, arrange these baby puds on large plates or trays, much like canapés, and hand them round.

Equipment

Tins and moulds

You may have some dishes already, perhaps liqueur glasses, a mini muffin tin, ovenproof ramekin dishes or demitasse coffee cups. Additional dishes can be bought from specialist cook shops, the chinaware section of a department store, or online. Small plastic shot glasses can be bought in packs from supermarkets.

The dishes used are between 50 ml/2 fl oz and 150 ml/5 fl oz. Where small silicone muffin trays are used, a measurement has been given for the base of the muffin cups; metal mini muffin trays with 12- or 24-section cups are also used for some recipes. The liqueur glasses used hold 50 ml/2 fl oz.

For traybake desserts you will need a 30 x 20 x 5-cm/ 12 x 8 x 2-inch loose-bottomed cake tin. For the triple chocolate mousses (see page 52) you will need a deep 20-cm/8-inch loose-bottomed square cake tin.

Mini desserts can be served in paper or foil petits fours or cupcake cases, or straight onto plates or mini cocktail paper napkins. Some can be served on forks or spoons.

Piping bags and nozzles

A large nylon or waxed cotton piping bag has been used with a selection of plain or star nozzles. This is essential for piping mini éclairs (see page 76) and some meringue (see page 40), and for filling mini chocolate cases or glasses without smears (see page 60).

For finer decorative work, greaseproof or non-stick baking paper piping bags can be shaped into a cone from a double-thickness triangle of paper, filled, then the tip snipped away with scissors, saving the need for smaller piping nozzles. Plastic disposable piping bags can be bought from specialist cookshops.

Cooking techniques

Freezing

If you are freezing desserts served in glasses, choose plastic glasses. Arrange the desserts on a baking tray or in a plastic box and freeze them uncovered until firm, then cover with cling film or the plastic box lid, seal and label. Use within 6 weeks. Defrost desserts in the fridge overnight or at room temperature for 2 hours, then transfer to the fridge. If the desserts have been frozen, do not return any leftover desserts to the freezer.

Gelatine

This book uses powdered gelatine. Scoop the powder into a measuring teaspoon so it is level with the spoon, then sprinkle it over cold water in a small heatproof bowl. If specks remain on the surface of the water, gently stir them in using a teaspoon. Allow the gelatine to soak for 5 minutes (it forms a sponge-like mixture), then stand the bowl in a small saucepan and pour water into the pan halfway up the bowl. Gently simmer the water for 5 minutes, until the gelatine melts and is a clear, straw-coloured liquid. If it gets very hot, allow it to cool for a few minutes. Trickle the gelatine into your wine, juice or cream. Pour the mixture straight into serving dishes (if the jelly contains sliced fruit, which may float, allow the jelly to partially set before adding it to the serving dishes). Chill in the fridge for 3–4 hours.

To turn a jelly out, dip a metal mould into just-boiled water for 2 seconds (longer if it is silicone), then loosen the top of the jelly with your fingertips and invert the mould onto a serving plate. Holding the mould and plate, give a quick jerk, remove the mould and clean the dish with kitchen paper. Serve within 30 minutes.

Caramel

The secret to caramel is to avoid stirring the sugar as it dissolves, as this can make it crystallize. Heat the sugar and water gently in a heavy-based saucepan, tilting it from time to time. Once the sugar has dissolved, boil rapidly for 4–5 minutes; the syrup will colour around the edges and then will burn easily, so do not leave the pan unattended. Tilt the pan gently to encourage even colouring. When browned remove from the heat.

Meringues

Always use a clean, dry bowl and whisk. Whisk the egg whites until they form stiff, moist-looking peaks, then tilt the bowl; they won't move if they are ready. Gradually whisk in the sugar, a teaspoonful at a time, then continue to whisk for 1–2 minutes after it has been added to make the mixture smooth, thickened and glossy. Spoon or pipe onto baking trays lined with non-stick baking paper and bake in a low oven, as specified in the recipe, until the meringues are crisp and can be lifted easily off the paper. If they are sticky on the base, cook for a few minutes longer, then try again. Cooled unfilled meringues will keep in a cool place in a biscuit tin layered with baking paper for 3–4 days.

Lining tins

For square tins, place the tin on non-stick baking paper, draw around it and cut out the paper inside the lines. Cut a strip of paper the depth of the tin and make a 1-cm/½-inch fold along one long edge. Grease the tin using a pastry brush, then fit the strip around the sides so the folded part sits on the base and snip the folded edge at the corners. Press the paper square into the base. For round-sectioned tins, grease the sections. Cut out circles of non-stick baking paper 1-cm/½-inch larger than the section diameters. Make 5-mm/¼-inch cuts at the sides of the circles and press them in so the snipped edges go up the sides.

Muffins and cupcakes

Muffins are made by adding the wet ingredients to the dry ones. The flour is usually sifted first. Add the wet ingredients all in one go and fold everything together gently. As soon as they're combined but with specks of flour still visible, spoon the mixture into the cases Over-mixing can make them heavy. Unless otherwise stated, fill cupcake cases until they're almost full and the mixture is level with the top of the cases. For muffins, the mixture can extend above the tops of the cases slightly to achieve the 'muffin top'.

How to tell if a cake is cooked

When cooked, cakes are usually domed in the centre with a lightly browned surface. Gently touch them with your fingers; they should feel just firm. Push a skewer into the centre; if cooked, it will come out clean.

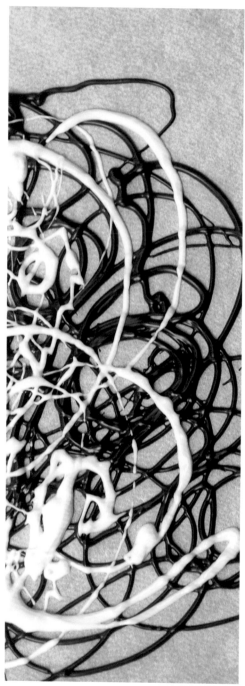

Decoration techniques

Chocolate curls

Spread just-melted chocolate over a marble pastry board or cheese board into a thin, even layer no less than 5-mm/¼-inch thick. Leave in a cool place to set. To make the curls, draw a long cook's knife across the chocolate at a 45° angle in a see-saw action to shave the chocolate into curls. For two-tone chocolate caraque, spread a band of melted white chocolate on the marble, leave to set for 5 minutes, then spread a band of melted dark chocolate onto it, butting up to the white chocolate, making sure that the level of the chocolate is the same for both types. Leave to set, then shave into curls as above.

For speedy chocolate curls, turn a block of chocolate over so that the smooth underside is uppermost, then place the block on a chopping board and run a vegetable peeler firmly over the surface so that the blade is at a slight angle to the chocolate. The size of the curl that you make will depend on the temperature of the chocolate and the amount of fat it contains. If the chocolate is very cold, the curls will be tiny, so soften it in the microwave at full power for 10 seconds (if the bar is large or the chocolate is dark, you may need to give it a second burst in the microwave). The fewer cocoa solids the chocolate contains, the easier it will be to shape, so white and milk chocolate will make larger curls than plain chocolate.

Piped chocolate

Spoon melted chocolate into a small non-stick baking paper piping bag (see page 6), roll down the top to enclose the chocolate, then snip a little off the tip of the bag. There is no need to add a piping nozzle. Pipe shapes such as leaves, flowers, butterflies, initials and hearts over non-stick baking paper freehand, or draw them on a second sheet of paper using a black pen, then slide it under the top sheet before piping. Fill in the shapes with extra piped squiggles of chocolate or flood the centre to fill completely.

Coloured chocolate

Melted white chocolate can be coloured with the tiniest amount of liquid food colouring and can make an eye-catching decoration piped over a layer of dark chocolate.

Sugar decorations

Ready-to-roll fondant icing can be left white or coloured with paste or gel food colourings before being shaped. Don't use liquid food colourings, as these will make the icing sticky and tricky to roll out. Paste or gel colours can be bought from supermarkets, specialist cookshops or online in a wide variety of colours. Apply the colouring to the icing on the end of a cocktail stick and use sparingly. Knead the colouring in, then roll the icing out thinly and stamp out stars, holly leaves, snowflakes or tiny hearts or flowers using cutters. (Look out for mini-plunger flower cutters, as these can be depressed into a small circle of foam for a curved flower effect). Allow the decorations to dry at room temperature on a tray lined with non-stick baking paper, then store them in a small plastic box, interleaved with extra paper, for up to 2 months. You can also buy ready-made sugar flowers or choose from a range of edible glitter, sugar strands or tiny shapes from supermarkets or specialist suppliers.

Natural flower decorations

Tiny flowers from the garden can add a delicate finishing touch to a miniature dessert, but first make sure that they are edible. Choose from tiny viola or pansy flowers in a mix of colours to borage, violet, little rose petals or herb flowers or tiny mint leaves. Brush petals or leaves lightly with a little beaten egg white, then sprinkle with caster sugar and allow to dry on a tray lined with non-stick baking paper for an hour. Use immediately.

Citrus curls

Pare away the rind from lemons, oranges or limes with a zester (a small metal-topped tool with a row of holes punched in the top). Dust the curls with a little caster sugar and sprinkle them over mousses or ice creams. For larger, corkscrew-type curls, remove the citrus peel in single, slightly larger strips with a canelle knife, then twist each strip tightly around a cocktail stick, leave for a minute, slide the cocktail stick out and hang the corkscrew curl over the edge of the serving dish.

Caramel shards

Just-cooked caramel can be drizzled over non-stick baking paper, then left to cool and harden. When ready to serve, break it into shards or chop it into small pieces. Chopped or flaked nuts can also be added before it hardens, for extra interest.

Mini Comfort Desserts

Blueberry and maple syrup pancakes

Makes: 30
Prep: 20 minutes
Cook: 10-15 minutes

Popular with diners of all ages, these bite-sized pancakes take only a few minutes to prepare – which is just as well, as the chances are they will disappear as soon as they are cooked.

175 g/6 oz plain flour

1 tsp baking powder

½ tsp bicarbonate of soda

1 tbsp caster sugar

2 eggs, separated

finely grated rind of 1 lemon and juice of ½ lemon

250 ml/9 fl oz milk

115 g/4 oz blueberries

a little sunflower oil, for frying

maple syrup, to serve

crème fraîche, to serve (optional)

1. Put the flour, baking powder and bicarbonate of soda into a mixing bowl, then stir in the sugar. Whisk the egg whites in a separate large, clean mixing bowl until you have soft peaks.

2. Add the egg yolks, lemon rind and lemon juice to the flour, then gradually whisk in the milk until smooth. Fold in a spoonful of the whisked egg whites, then add the rest and fold in gently. Sprinkle the blueberries into the bowl, then gently and briefly fold them in.

3. Pour a little oil into a large frying pan, then place it over a medium heat. When it's hot, drop dessertspoonfuls of the blueberry mixture into the pan, leaving a little space between the pancakes. Cook for 2–3 minutes, until bubbles appear on the surface of the pancakes and the undersides are golden. Turn the pancakes over and cook the second side for 1–2 minutes, until golden.

4. Remove the pancakes from the pan using a palette knife and keep them hot in a clean tea towel. Cook the remaining blueberry mixture in batches of 10 pancakes at a time, until all the mixture is cooked, oiling the pan as needed.

5. Transfer the pancakes to small dessert plates, serving 4–5 pancakes per portion. Drizzle a little maple syrup over them and serve extra syrup in a small jug. Top the pancakes with teaspoonfuls of crème fraîche if liked.

Cherry and almond bakes

Makes: 18
Prep: 25 minutes
Cook: 12–15 minutes

Make these cakes when cherries are in season, or cheat and use canned cherries that have been well drained. Serve them still warm from the oven, with a little dish of crème fraîche on the side if you like.

55 g/2 oz unsalted butter, softened, plus extra for greasing

55 g/2 oz caster sugar

55 g/2 oz self-raising flour

25 g/1 oz ground almonds

1 egg

a few drops of almond extract

18 fresh cherries, stalked and stoned, or 18 canned cherries

25 g/1 oz flaked almonds

icing sugar, sifted, for dusting

crème fraîche, to serve (optional)

1. Preheat the oven to 180°C/350°F/Gas Mark 4. Lightly grease 18 sections of 2 x 12-section mini muffin tins with butter.

2. Put the butter, sugar, flour and ground almonds into a mixing bowl, then stir. Add the egg and almond extract and beat together briefly using a wooden spoon, until smooth.

3. Spoon the mixture into the muffin tin sections, then lightly press a cherry into the centre of each cake. Sprinkle with the flaked almonds. Bake in the preheated oven for 12–15 minutes, or until risen and firm to the touch.

4. Leave the cakes in the tin for 5 minutes, then loosen with a round-bladed knife and transfer to a wire rack to cool. Serve warm, dusted with sifted icing sugar, with spoonfuls of crème fraîche if liked.

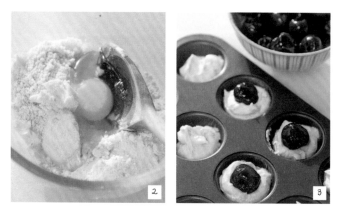

Berry and oat crumbles

Makes: 8
Prep: 20 minutes
Cook: 20 minutes

These homely little puddings are always a great hit. If you wish, make double the amount of crumble topping and store it in the freezer, then use it at a later date and bake from frozen.

450 g/1 lb red plums, halved, stoned and diced

115 g/4 oz raspberries

25 g/1 oz light muscovado sugar

3 tbsp water

ready-made custard, to serve

TOPPING

85 g/3 oz plain flour

20 g/¾ oz porridge oats

20 g/¾ oz barley flakes

40 g/1½ oz light muscovado sugar

40 g/1½ oz unsalted butter, chilled and diced

1. Preheat the oven to 180°C/350°F/Gas Mark 4. Put the plums, raspberries, 25 g/1 oz sugar and water into a heavy-based saucepan. Cover and simmer for 5 minutes, or until the fruit has softened.

2. For the topping, put the flour, porridge oats, barley flakes and sugar into a mixing bowl and stir. Rub in the butter using your fingertips until the mixture resembles fine crumbs.

3. Spoon the fruit mixture into 8 x 150-ml/5-fl oz metal pudding moulds and stand them on a baking tray. Sprinkle the topping on top.

4. Bake in the preheated oven for 15 minutes, or until golden. Allow the crumbles to cool for 5–10 minutes, then serve topped with small spoonfuls of custard.

Cinnamon and apple fritters with blackberry sauce

Makes: 30
Prep: 30 minutes
Cook: 20–35 minutes

A retro dessert that uses storecupboard ingredients. It's a good way to make the most of blackberries you have in the freezer. Alternatively, use whatever frozen berries you have to hand – raspberries or blackcurrants would work well.

8 small dessert apples

150 g/5½ oz blackberries

125 ml/4 fl oz water

6 tbsp caster sugar

150 g/5½ oz plain flour

a large pinch of ground cinnamon

1 egg, separated

150 ml/5 fl oz milk

1 litre/1¾ pints sunflower oil

1. For the sauce, quarter, core, peel and dice 2 of the apples, then put them into a heavy-based saucepan. Add the blackberries, water and 1 tablespoon of the sugar. Cover and simmer for 5–10 minutes, or until the apples have softened. Purée until smooth using a handheld blender, then press through a sieve into a serving bowl to remove the seeds. Cover with cling film and set aside.

2. Peel and core the remaining apples, cut them into thin rings, then put them in a plastic bag with 40 g/1½ oz of the flour. Seal the bag, then shake to coat the apples thinly with the flour.

3. Put the remaining flour into a mixing bowl. Stir in 1 tablespoon of the sugar, the cinnamon and the egg yolk. Gradually whisk in the milk until smooth.

4. Whisk the egg white in a separate large, clean mixing bowl until you have soft peaks. Fold it into the flour mixture.

5. Pour the oil into a saucepan, making sure that it is no more than half full. Heat to 160°C/325°F on a sugar thermometer, or until bubbles form when a little batter is dropped into the oil. Line a plate with kitchen paper.

6. Shake any excess flour from the apple slices, then dip them into the batter and remove them using 2 forks. Drain off the excess batter, then carefully add 4–5 apple slices to the hot oil and cook for 2–3 minutes, or until golden. Lift out of the oil with a draining spoon, then transfer to the lined plate and leave to drain while you cook the remaining apples in batches of this size.

7. Sprinkle the remaining sugar over the fritters and serve with the blackberry sauce for dipping.

S'mores

Makes: 18
Prep: 25 minutes
Cook: 12–15 minutes

An American and Canadian treat that is traditionally cooked over a campfire. This recipe uses homemade buttery cookies sandwiched with marshmallows and topped with melting chocolate.

a little sunflower oil, for greasing

175 g/6 oz wholewheat flour, plus extra for dusting

2 tsp baking powder

55 g/2 oz medium oatmeal

55 g/2 oz caster sugar

150 g/5½ oz unsalted butter, chilled and diced

2 egg yolks

200 g/7 oz plain chocolate, broken into 18 pieces

18 marshmallows

1. Preheat the oven to 180°C/350°F/Gas Mark 4. Lightly brush 2 baking trays with oil.

2. Put the flour, baking powder, oatmeal and sugar into a mixing bowl, then stir. Rub in the butter using your fingertips until the mixture resembles fine crumbs. Stir in the egg yolks and press together using your hands to make a ball of dough.

3. Lightly dust a work surface with flour. Knead the dough lightly, then roll it out thinly. Stamp out 6-cm/2¼-inch circles using a biscuit cutter and transfer to the prepared baking trays. Shape the remaining dough into a ball, knead it, then roll it out thinly again and stamp out more biscuits. Continue until all the dough has been used up.

4. Bake in the preheated oven for 12–15 minutes, or until golden brown, then leave to cool a little.

5. Add a piece of chocolate to half the hot biscuits and a marshmallow to the other half. Leave for 1–2 minutes, or until the chocolate just begins to melt, then sandwich the biscuits together in pairs so that the marshmallows are in the centre and the chocolate on top. Serve warm or cold.

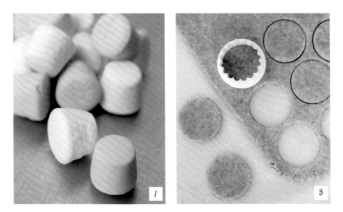

Hot orange soufflés with chocolate and orange sauce

Makes: 12
Prep: 25 minutes
Cook: 20–25 minutes

Serving hot soufflés adds a touch of theatre to any meal as they puff up dramatically in the oven but fall just as quickly. Get your dinner guests ready and waiting, dust the tops of the soufflés with a speedy flourish of icing sugar, then serve, hopefully, to applause.

25 g/1 oz unsalted butter, for greasing

115 g/4 oz caster sugar, plus 2 tbsp for sprinkling

3 eggs, separated, plus 1 extra egg white

40 g/1½ oz plain flour

225 ml/8 fl oz milk

finely grated rind of 1 large orange

5 tbsp orange juice, or 3 tbsp orange juice plus 2 tbsp Cointreau

a large pinch of ground cinnamon

icing sugar, sifted, for dusting

SAUCE

150 g/5½ oz plain chocolate, roughly chopped

4 tbsp orange juice

2 tbsp caster sugar

1. Grease 12 x 125-ml/4-fl oz wide-topped ovenproof demitasse coffee cups with the butter, then sprinkle them with 2 tablespoons of caster sugar, tilting to coat them evenly. Put them on a baking tray and set aside.

2. Put half the measured sugar and all the egg yolks into a mixing bowl and beat together for 2 minutes using an electric handheld whisk, until thick and pale. Sift the flour over the surface, then fold it in.

3. Pour the milk into a medium heavy-based saucepan, bring just to the boil, then gradually whisk it into the egg mixture until smooth. Pour the mixture back into the pan, then cook over a low heat, whisking gently, until thickened and smooth.

4. Remove the soufflé mixture from the heat and whisk in the orange rind, juice, Cointreau if using, and cinnamon. Cover with cling film and leave to cool.

5. Preheat the oven to 190°C/375°F/Gas Mark 5. Whisk the egg whites in a large, clean mixing bowl until you have stiff, moist-looking peaks. Gradually whisk in the remaining sugar, a teaspoonful at a time. Fold the whites into the cooled soufflé mixture, then divide between the 12 dishes so that they are three-quarters full. Bake in the preheated oven for 15–20 minutes, or until the soufflés are well risen, the tops are golden and they are almost set in the centre.

6. Meanwhile, to make the sauce, put the chocolate, orange juice and sugar in a heatproof bowl, set the bowl over a saucepan of gently simmering water and heat until smooth and melted, stirring from time to time. Pour into a jug.

7. Quickly serve the soufflés on saucers, dust with sifted icing sugar and drizzle the warm chocolate sauce over the top.

Cranberry and granola sundaes

Makes: 10
Prep: 20 minutes
Cook: 13–15 minutes

With the mix of tangy, slightly sharp cranberry compote, creamy smooth Greek yogurt and crunchy granola, this is a great dessert or party brunch. Make up extra granola and serve in little dishes as an alternative to crisps.

a little sunflower oil, for greasing

2 tbsp sesame seeds

2 tbsp pumpkin seeds

25 g/1 oz porridge oats

25 g/1 oz flaked almonds

40 g/1½ oz unsalted butter

2 tbsp runny honey

2 tbsp light muscovado sugar

250 g/9 oz honey-flavoured Greek yogurt

CRANBERRY COMPOTE

2 tsp cornflour

85 g/3 oz light muscovado sugar

juice of 1 large orange

200 g/7 oz frozen cranberries

1. Preheat the oven to 180°C/350°F/Gas Mark 4. Lightly brush a large baking tray with oil.

2. Put the sesame seeds, pumpkin seeds, porridge oats and flaked almonds into a bowl and mix together using your fingertips. Put the butter, honey and sugar into a heavy-based saucepan and heat gently until the butter has melted and the sugar dissolved. Remove from the heat and stir in the seed mixture. Tip onto the prepared baking tray and spread into a thin, even layer. Bake in the preheated oven for 8–10 minutes, stirring halfway through cooking and moving the browned edges to the centre. Allow to cool in the tin.

3. For the cranberry compote, put the cornflour, sugar and orange juice into a heavy-based saucepan and cook over a medium heat, stirring, until smooth. Add the frozen cranberries and cook, uncovered, for 5 minutes, stirring, until they have softened and the juices have thickened. Allow to cool.

4. Crumble half the granola using your fingertips and break the rest into shards. Sprinkle a layer of the crumble into 10 shot glasses, spoon on a layer of yogurt, then a layer of cranberry compote. Repeat the layers, finishing with a layer of compote, and decorate with the shards of granola. Any remaining granola shards can be served in a small separate dish.

Chocolate fondants with toffee sauce

Makes: 10
Prep: 25 minutes
Chill: 1 hour or overnight
Cook: 17–20 minutes

This restaurant favourite is surprisingly easy to make and can be prepared in advance then left in the fridge for up to 24 hours. The secret is to bake the puddings for precisely the cooking time and test one before serving them. They should be crusty on top but soft and molten in the centre.

150 g/5½ oz unsalted butter

4 tsp cocoa powder

150 g/5½ oz plain chocolate, roughly chopped

2 eggs, plus 2 egg yolks

125 g/4½ oz caster sugar

25 g/1 oz plain flour

icing sugar, sifted, for dusting

TOFFEE SAUCE

55 g/2 oz unsalted butter

55 g/2 oz light muscovado sugar

1 tbsp runny honey

150 ml/5 fl oz double cream

1. Melt 25 g/1 oz of the butter in a small saucepan, then brush it over the insides of 10 x 125-ml/4-fl oz ovenproof ramekins. Sift a little cocoa into each ramekin, then tilt to coat the base and sides evenly, tapping out any excess.

2. Put the chocolate and remaining 125 g/4½ oz butter in a heatproof bowl, set the bowl over a saucepan of gently simmering water and heat until melted, stirring from time to time.

3. Put the eggs, egg yolks and caster sugar into a mixing bowl and whisk together until thick and frothy and the whisk leaves a trail when raised above the mixture. Sift over the flour, then gently fold it in.

4. Fold the melted chocolate mixture into the egg mixture until smooth. Pour it into the prepared ramekins, cover and chill in the fridge for 1 hour, or overnight if time allows.

5. For the toffee sauce, put the butter, light muscovado sugar and honey into a heavy-based saucepan and heat gently for 3–4 minutes, or until the butter has melted and the sugar dissolved, then boil for 1–2 minutes, stirring, until it begins to smell of toffee and thicken. Remove from the heat and stir in the cream.

6. Preheat the oven to 180°C/350°F/Gas Mark 4. Take the ramekins out of the fridge and leave at room temperature for 10 minutes. Bake in the preheated oven for 10–12 minutes, or until well risen, the tops are crusty and the centres still slightly soft. Reheat the sauce over a low heat, if needed.

7. Dust the desserts with sifted icing sugar. Serve with the sauce in a jug for guests to pour on.

Mini Indulgent Desserts

Raspberry and strawberry pavlovas

Makes: 20
Prep: 25 minutes
Cook: 25–30 minutes

Spoil the ones you love with these gorgeous-looking meringues. You can make them in advance and keep them in an airtight tin for several days, then just make the topping when you are ready to serve them.

2 egg whites

115 g/4 oz caster sugar

½ tsp cornflour

½ tsp white wine vinegar

TOPPING

300 ml/10 fl oz double cream

finely grated rind and juice of
1 lime

3 tbsp strawberry jam

200 g/7 oz raspberries

200 g/7 oz small strawberries,
hulled and sliced

1. Preheat the oven to 140°C/275°F/Gas Mark 1. Line a large baking tray with non-stick baking paper.

2. Whisk the egg whites in a large, clean mixing bowl until you have stiff, moist-looking peaks. Gradually whisk in the sugar a tablespoonful at a time. Once all the sugar has been added, whisk for a further 1–2 minutes, until the meringue is thick and glossy.

3. Mix the cornflour and vinegar together in a small bowl until smooth, then fold it into the meringue. Spoon the mixture onto the prepared baking tray in 20 mounds, leaving a little space between each mound. Spread it into circles 5 cm/2 inches in diameter, then make a small dip in the centre of each circle using the back of a teaspoon.

4. Bake in the preheated oven for 25–30 minutes, or until the meringues are a very pale biscuit colour and can easily be lifted off the paper. If they stick to the paper, cook them for a few minutes longer, then retest. Leave to cool on the paper.

5. For the topping, pour the cream into a large mixing bowl and whisk until it forms soft swirls, then fold in the lime rind. Spoon a dollop of the cream onto the top of each pavlova, then transfer to a serving plate.

6. Put the jam and lime juice in a small heavy-based saucepan and place over a gentle heat until the jam has just melted. Stir in the raspberries and strawberries, then leave to cool a little. Spoon the fruit over the pavlovas and serve.

Strawberry and rosé jellies

Makes: 8
Prep: 20 minutes
Cook: 5 minutes
Chill: 4 hours

A pretty finale to any summer celebration. If you have roses in the garden you may like to decorate the cream with tiny pink rose petals instead of finely grated lemon rind.

150 g/5½ oz small strawberries, hulled and sliced

1½ tbsp caster sugar

3 tbsp water

2 tsp powdered gelatine

200 ml/7 fl oz rosé wine

TOPPING

1½ tbsp caster sugar

2 tbsp rosé wine

finely grated rind of 1 lemon

150 ml/5 fl oz double cream

1. Put the strawberries and sugar into a mixing bowl and mix together using a metal spoon.

2. Put the water in a small heatproof bowl, then sprinkle the gelatine over the surface, making sure the powder is absorbed. Set aside for 5 minutes. Set the bowl of gelatine in a saucepan of gently simmering water and heat for about 5 minutes, stirring from time to time, until the gelatine is a clear liquid (see page 7).

3. Divide the sugar-coated strawberries between 8 small champagne or liqueur glasses. Pour the 200 ml/7 fl oz wine into a measuring jug and stir in the gelatine, then pour it into the glasses. Cover and chill in the fridge for 4 hours, or until the jelly has set.

4. To make the topping, put the sugar, wine and half the lemon rind into a small bowl and stir. Pour the cream into a large mixing bowl and whisk until it forms soft swirls. Add the wine mixture and whisk briefly, until the cream is thick again. Spoon the lemon cream into the centre of the jellies, then decorate with the remaining lemon rind.

Rippled raspberry cheesecakes

Makes: 12
Prep: 30 minutes
Cook: 5 minutes
Chill: 3 hours

55 g/2 oz unsalted butter

115 g/4 oz digestives or graham crackers, crushed

3 tbsp water

2 tsp powdered gelatine

150 g/5½ oz raspberries, plus 24 to decorate

150 ml/5 fl oz double cream

150 ml/5 fl oz ready-made custard

¼ tsp vanilla extract

Silicone trays make turning out these dainty desserts child's play. The swirled effect is simple to create but looks really impressive.

1. Melt the butter in a saucepan, then stir in the biscuit crumbs. Divide the mixture between the sections of 2 x 6-section silicone muffin trays; the base of each cup should be 4 cm/1½ inches in diameter. Press over the base of the sections using the back of a teaspoon, then chill in the fridge.

2. Put the water in a small heatproof bowl, then sprinkle the gelatine over the surface, making sure the powder is absorbed. Set aside for 5 minutes. Meanwhile, purée the 150 g/5½ oz raspberries in a blender, then press through a sieve into a bowl to remove the seeds. Set the bowl of gelatine in a saucepan of gently simmering water and heat for about 5 minutes, stirring from time to time, until the gelatine is a clear liquid (see page 7).

3. Pour the cream into a large mixing bowl and whisk until it forms soft swirls. Fold in the custard and vanilla. Stir 1½ tablespoons of the gelatine into the raspberry purée and fold the rest into the cream mixture. Spoon the cream mixture into the muffin trays, level the surface using the back of a teaspoon, then spoon the raspberry purée on top. Swirl the two mixtures together using the handle of the teaspoon. Cover and chill in the fridge for 3 hours, or longer if time allows, until set.

4. To serve, loosen the desserts using a round-bladed knife, then turn them out by pressing underneath. Decorate each dessert with 2 raspberries.

Lemon and blueberry duets

Makes: 10
Prep: 15 minutes
Cook: 5 minutes
Chill: 1–2 hours

300 ml/10 fl oz double cream

90 g/3¼ oz caster sugar

finely grated rind and juice of
1 lemon, plus grated rind of
1 lemon to decorate

1 tsp cornflour

4 tbsp water

250 g/9 oz blueberries

If you need a pudding in a hurry, then this is it. It takes just 20 minutes to make, then can be left in the fridge to chill until you are ready to serve.

1. Put the cream and 75 g/2¾ oz sugar into a medium heavy-based saucepan, then heat gently, stirring, until the sugar has dissolved. Increase the heat and bring to the boil, then cook for 1 minute, stirring.

2. Remove from the heat, add half the finely grated lemon rind and all the juice, and stir continuously for 1 minute, until the mixture begins to thicken slightly. Pour into 10 shot glasses, then leave to cool.

3. Put the remaining sugar and finely grated lemon rind into a smaller heavy-based saucepan, stir in the cornflour, then gradually mix in the water until smooth. Add half the blueberries, then place over a medium heat and cook, stirring, for 3–4 minutes, until they are starting to soften and the sauce thicken.

4. Remove the compote from the heat, stir in the remaining blueberries, then leave to cool. Cover the glasses and blueberry compote with cling film, then transfer to the fridge for 1–2 hours, or until set.

5. When ready to serve, stir the blueberries, then spoon them into the glasses and decorate with the grated lemon rind.

White chocolate and strawberry cheesecakes

Makes: 40
Prep: 30 minutes
Cook: 45–50 minutes
Chill: overnight

An all-American favourite, this baked cheesecake tastes even better the day after it is made.

SPONGE

55 g/2 oz margarine, softened

55 g/2 oz caster sugar

55 g/2 oz self-raising flour

1 egg

CHEESECAKE

200 g/7 oz white chocolate, roughly chopped

600 g/1lb 5 oz full-fat soft cheese

85 g/3 oz caster sugar

1 tsp vanilla extract

200 ml/7 fl oz double cream

4 eggs

TOPPING

250 ml/9 fl oz crème fraîche

10 strawberries, hulled and quartered

55 g/2 oz white chocolate, cut into shards using a swivel vegetable peeler

1. Preheat the oven to 180°C/350°F/Gas Mark 4. Line a 30 x 20 x 5-cm/ 12 x 8 x 2-inch loose-bottomed cake tin with non-stick baking paper, snipping diagonally into the corners, then pressing the paper into the tin so that the base and sides are lined.

2. Put all the sponge ingredients into a mixing bowl and beat together using a wooden spoon until smooth. Spoon the mixture into the prepared tin and spread it into a thin layer using a spatula. Bake in the preheated oven for 10–12 minutes, or until golden and firm to the touch. Remove from the oven and leave to cool. Reduce the oven temperature to 150°C/300°F/Gas Mark 2.

3. For the cheesecake, put the chocolate in a heatproof bowl, set the bowl over a saucepan of gently simmering water and heat until melted. Stir briefly and leave to cool. Meanwhile, put the soft cheese, sugar and vanilla extract into a mixing bowl and beat together briefly using an electric handheld whisk until just smooth. Gradually beat in the cream until thick once more. Beat in the eggs one at a time, waiting until the mixture is smooth before adding the next one. Stir in the melted chocolate.

4. Spoon the cheesecake mixture onto the sponge and spread it out so it forms an even layer. Bake in the preheated oven for 30–35 minutes, or until the edge is slightly cracked and the centre still a little soft. Turn off the oven, leave the door ajar and leave to cool.

5. Cover the cheesecake and put it in the fridge overnight. When ready to serve, remove the cheesecake from the tin, peel off the baking paper and cut into 40 squares. Put these on a serving plate and top each square with a spoonful of crème fraîche. Add a quarter of a strawberry to each square and sprinkle with white chocolate shards.

Apricot and chocolate meringues

Makes: 12
Prep: 20 minutes
Cook: 10–13 minutes

Quick and easy to make, these pretty puddings look lovely served on a plate or platter. When apricots are out of season, try making these with halved plums.

6 apricots, halved and stoned

juice of ½ small orange

1 egg white

2 tbsp caster sugar

40 g/1½ oz plain chocolate, cut into 12 pieces

1. Preheat the oven to 180°C/350°F/Gas Mark 4.

2. Arrange the apricots, cut side up, on a baking tray. Drizzle the orange juice over the top of them. Bake in the preheated oven for 5–8 minutes.

3. Meanwhile, whisk the egg white in a large, clean mixing bowl until you have stiff, moist-looking peaks. Gradually whisk in the sugar a teaspoonful at a time. Once all the sugar has been added, whisk for a further 1–2 minutes, until the meringue is thick and glossy.

4. Spoon the meringue into a piping bag fitted with a medium star nozzle. Put a piece of chocolate in the centre of each apricot.

5. If the apricots wobble, stick them to the baking tray with a little meringue. Pipe a whirl of meringue on top of the chocolate. Bake in the preheated oven for 5 minutes, or until the meringue is tinged golden brown and just cooked. Allow to cool for a few minutes, then transfer to a serving plate.

Baby blueberry brûlées

Makes: 12
Prep: 20 minutes
Cook: 15 minutes
Chill: 3–4 hours

This is a girlie pudding, in health-conscious-sized portions – although it will be hard to resist the temptation of second helpings!

125 g/4½ oz blueberries

4 egg yolks

1 tsp vanilla extract

100 g/3½ oz caster sugar

300 ml/10 fl oz double cream

1. Preheat the oven to 160°C/325°F/Gas Mark 3. Put 12 x 50-ml/2-fl oz ovenproof dishes in a large roasting tin and divide the blueberries between them.

2. Put the egg yolks, vanilla and 40 g/1½ oz sugar into a jug and mix together using a fork until smooth and creamy. Pour the cream into a small heavy-based saucepan, bring to the boil, then gradually mix it into the yolks. Strain the mixture through a sieve back into the pan before pouring it back into the jug.

3. Pour the cream mixture over the blueberries. Pour warm water into the roasting tin to come halfway up the sides of the dishes. Bake in the preheated oven for 15 minutes, or until the custard is just set, with a slight wobble in the centre.

4. Allow to cool for 5–10 minutes, then lift the dishes out of the water and transfer to the fridge to chill for 3–4 hours.

5. To serve, sprinkle the remaining sugar over the dishes in an even layer, then caramelize it using a cook's blow torch or under a grill preheated to hot.

Chocolate and ginger fridge cake

Makes: 36
Prep: 25 minutes
Cook: 6-7 minutes
Chill: 3-4 hours

For those moments when you really need a chocolate fix, this no-bake dessert fits the bill. Rich, dark and supremely chocolatey, it has a hint of ginger that contrasts well with the crunch of crushed biscuits.

55 g/2 oz hazelnuts

200 g/7 oz plain chocolate, roughly chopped

100 g/3½ oz unsalted butter

400 g/14 oz canned sweetened full-fat condensed milk

225 g/8 oz digestives or graham crackers, crushed

150 g/5½ oz ready-to-eat dried apricots, diced

55 g/2 oz stem ginger from a jar, drained and finely chopped

55 g/2 oz milk chocolate, roughly chopped

1. Line a shallow 20-cm/8-inch square cake tin with non-stick baking paper, snipping diagonally into the corners, then pressing the paper into the tin so that the base and sides are lined. Preheat the grill to medium. Put the hazelnuts on a baking tray and toast under the grill for 3-4 minutes, or until golden, shaking them halfway through.

2. Put the plain chocolate, butter and condensed milk into a heavy-based saucepan and heat very gently, stirring all the time, until the chocolate and butter have melted. Spoon 150 g/5½ oz of the mixture into a bowl, cover and set aside.

3. Put the toasted hazelnuts, biscuit crumbs, dried apricots and stem ginger into the remaining chocolate mixture, then stir well. Tip the mixture into the prepared cake tin and press it into an even layer.

4. Spoon the reserved chocolate mixture over the top of the fridge cake in a thin, even layer, then chill in the fridge for 3 hours, or until set.

5. Put the milk chocolate in a heatproof bowl, set the bowl over a saucepan of gently simmering water and heat until melted, then stir. Put the melted chocolate into a paper piping bag and snip off the tip, then pipe swirls onto the fridge cake (see page 8). Chill in the fridge for 15 minutes, then lift the cake out of the tin, peel off the paper and cut into 36 squares.

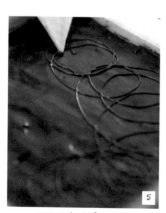

5

Mini Special Occasion Desserts

Berry torte

Makes: 20
Prep: 40 minutes
Cook: 25–30 minutes

Spoil the ones you love with these dainty, rich, dark-chocolate cakes layered with minty strawberries and swirled with rich chocolate cream. If you don't have a heart-shaped biscuit cutter, use a small round one instead.

85 g/3 oz cocoa powder

250 ml/9 fl oz boiling water

115 g/4 oz unsalted butter, softened

250 g/9 oz light muscovado sugar

2 eggs, beaten

200 g/7 oz plain flour

1 tsp baking powder

FILLING

150 ml/5 fl oz double cream

115 g/4 oz strawberries, hulled and finely chopped

1 tbsp finely chopped fresh mint

1 tbsp caster sugar

FROSTING

150 ml/5 fl oz double cream

150 g/5½ oz plain chocolate, roughly chopped

1. Preheat the oven to 180°C/350°F/Gas Mark 4. Line a deep 25-cm/10-inch square loose-bottomed cake tin with non-stick baking paper, snipping diagonally into the corners, then pressing the paper into the tin so that the base and sides are lined.

2. Put the cocoa in a heatproof bowl, then gradually stir in the boiling water until you have a smooth paste. Leave to cool.

3. Put the butter and light muscovado sugar into a mixing bowl and beat together using an electric handheld whisk until light and fluffy. Gradually beat in the eggs and a tablespoon of flour, until smooth. Sift the remaining flour and the baking powder into the bowl and fold them in, then gradually stir in the cooled cocoa mixture.

4. Pour the mixture into the prepared cake tin and spread into an even layer using a spatula. Bake in the preheated oven for 25–30 minutes, or until risen and firm to the touch and a skewer inserted into the centre of the cake comes out clean. Leave to cool for 10 minutes, then transfer to a wire rack and leave to cool completely.

5. Remove the baking paper and, using a 5-cm/2-inch heart-shaped cutter, cut out 20 cakes. Cut each cake in half horizontally.

6. For the filling, pour the cream into a large mixing bowl and whisk until it forms soft swirls. Fold in the strawberries, mint and caster sugar, then spread the mixture over the bottom half of each cake and top with the other cake half. Put the cakes on a wire rack.

7. For the frosting, pour the cream into a small heavy-based saucepan and bring just to the boil. Remove from the heat and add the chocolate. Set aside for 5 minutes, then stir until smooth and glossy. Allow to cool for a further 15 minutes, until thick, then spoon onto, and spread over, the top of the cakes. Leave to set, then transfer to a serving plate.

Strawberry and mint ice cream cones

Makes: 24
Prep: 40 minutes
Cook: 15-20 minutes
Freeze: 6 hours 20 minutes

These pretty cones would be fun to serve at a family summer party. Keep a few in the freezer for a very special dollies' tea party to thrill any little girl and her friends.

CONES

55 g/2 oz unsalted butter

2 egg whites

115 g/4 oz caster sugar

a few drops of vanilla extract

55 g/2 oz plain flour

ICE CREAM

115 g/4 oz caster sugar

6 tbsp water

2 sprigs of mint

450 g/1 lb strawberries, hulled and sliced, plus extra to serve

3 tsp powdered gelatine

150 ml/5 fl oz double cream

1. Preheat the oven to 180°C/350°F/Gas Mark 4. Line 3 baking trays with non-stick baking paper. You will need 8 metal cream horn tins or homemade cones made out of cardboard covered with baking paper to use as moulds.

2. For the cones, melt the butter in a saucepan. Lightly whisk the egg whites in a large, clean mixing bowl until frothy but still translucent. Whisk in the sugar, then the melted butter and the vanilla. Sift in the flour, then fold it in until smooth. Drop 4-5 half-teaspoonfuls of the mixture over one of the prepared baking trays and spread each into a circle 5-6 cm/2-2½ inches in diameter. Bake in the preheated oven for 3-5 minutes, or until just golden at the edges.

3. Allow the baked biscuits to harden for a few moments, then loosen with a palette knife and quickly shape into small cones around the moulds. Leave to set for 1-2 minutes, then remove the moulds. Repeat baking and shaping cones until all the mixture is used up, then leave to cool. Don't bake too many biscuits at once, or they will harden before you can shape them.

4. For the ice cream, put the sugar, 2 tablespoons of water and the mint into a medium heavy-based saucepan. Heat gently, stirring from time to time, until the sugar has dissolved. Add the sliced strawberries, increase the heat slightly and cook for 3 minutes. Discard the mint, then purée the mixture in a blender until smooth. Press the purée through a sieve into a metal loaf tin.

5. Put the remaining water in a small heatproof bowl, then sprinkle the gelatine over the surface, making sure the powder is absorbed. Set aside for 5 minutes. Set the bowl of gelatine in a saucepan of gently simmering water and heat for about 5 minutes, stirring from time to time, until the gelatine is a clear liquid (see page 7). Gently stir the gelatine into the puréed strawberry mixture, leave to cool, then freeze for 20 minutes.

6. Pour the cream in a large mixing bowl and whisk until it forms soft swirls. Transfer the just-setting strawberry mixture to another large mixing bowl and whisk for a few minutes. Fold the cream into the strawberries. Stand the cones in small cups and pipe the ice cream into them. Freeze for 6 hours or overnight. To serve, arrange the cones in a glass bowl with extra strawberries.

Triple chocolate mousses

Makes: 36
Prep: 45 minutes
Cook: 2 minutes
Chill: overnight
Freeze: 45 minutes

These smart-looking desserts can be prepared the day before you plan to serve them, or even frozen, and are easier to slice if not fully defrosted.

55 g/2 oz unsalted butter

1 tbsp cocoa powder

150 g/5½ oz digestives or graham crackers, crushed

milk chocolate curls, to decorate

MOUSSE

4 tbsp water

4 tsp powdered gelatine

115 g/4 oz plain chocolate, roughly chopped

115 g/4 oz milk chocolate, roughly chopped

115 g/4 oz white chocolate, roughly chopped

125 g/4½ oz unsalted butter

6 tbsp milk

6 eggs, separated

½ tsp vanilla extract

350 ml/12 fl oz double cream

1. Line a deep 20-cm/8-inch square loose-bottomed cake tin with 2 long strips of cling film, laid over each other in a cross, then press into the tin. The edges of the cling film should hang over the sides of the tin.

2. Melt the butter in a small saucepan, then stir in the cocoa and biscuit crumbs. Press the mixture into the tin in an even layer, then cover and chill in the fridge.

3. For the mousse, put the water in a small heatproof bowl, then sprinkle the gelatine over the surface, making sure the powder is absorbed. Set aside for 5 minutes. Set the bowl of gelatine in a saucepan of gently simmering water and heat for 5 mintes, stirring from time to time, until the gelatine is a clear liquid (see page 7).

4. Put each type of chopped chocolate in a different heatproof bowl, then add one-third of the butter and 2 tablespoons of milk to each bowl. Place each bowl over a saucepan of gently simmering water and heat until the chocolate has melted. Stir 2 egg yolks into each bowl one at a time then remove from the heat.

5. Stir 4 teaspoons of the dissolved gelatine into each bowl, then stir the vanilla into the white chocolate. Pour the cream into a fourth bowl and whisk until it forms soft swirls. Fold one-third of the cream into each of the chocolate mixtures. Whisk the egg whites in a large, clean mixing bowl until you have soft peaks, then divide them between the chocolate bowls and fold in gently.

6. Pour the plain chocolate mousse into the biscuit-lined tin, spread it into an even layer, then freeze for 15 minutes. Spoon over the white chocolate layer and freeze for 30 minutes. Gently whisk the milk chocolate layer to soften, if needed, then spoon it over and chill in the fridge overnight, or until set.

7. To serve, lift the mousse out of the tin, pressing from the base. Peel off the cling film. Cut the mousse into 6 strips using a wet knife, then cut each strip into 6 small squares, wiping and wetting the knife frequently so that the layers don't become smeared. Arrange on small plates or saucers and decorate with milk chocolate curls.

Shortbread stacks

Makes: 24
Prep: 40 minutes
Cook: 13-15 minutes

Make the shortbread biscuits and fruit compotes a day ahead of serving, then assemble the stacks just before you need them. For a baby's christening or birthday, sprinkle the tops with pink or blue sugar confetti or tiny icing shapes.

250 ml/9 fl oz crème fraîche

icing sugar, sifted, for dusting

SHORTBREAD

150 g/5½ oz plain flour, plus extra for dusting

25 g/1 oz cornflour

55 g/2 oz caster sugar, plus extra for sprinkling

finely grated rind of 1 lemon

115 g/4 oz unsalted butter, chilled and diced

FRUIT COMPOTES

2 tsp cornflour

55 g/2 oz caster sugar

juice of 1 lemon

150 g/5½ oz blueberries, plus 12 to decorate

150 g/5½ oz raspberries, plus 12 to decorate

1. Preheat the oven to 160°C/325°F/Gas Mark 3.

2. For the shortbread, put the flour, cornflour, sugar and lemon rind into a mixing bowl and stir together. Rub in the butter using your fingertips until the mixture resembles fine crumbs. Press together using your hands to make a ball of dough. Lightly dust a work surface with flour.

3. Knead the dough lightly, then cut it in half and roll out each half thinly. Stamp out 4.5-cm/1¾-inch flower shapes or fluted circles using a biscuit cutter and transfer to a non-stick baking tray. Add the trimmings to the reserved dough and roll it out thinly, then stamp out more biscuits and transfer them to another baking tray. Continue until all the dough has been used; you should have at least 72 biscuits. Sprinkle with extra sugar, then bake in the preheated oven for 8–10 minutes, or until pale golden. Leave to cool on the trays.

4. To make the fruit compotes, divide the cornflour, sugar and lemon juice equally between 2 small heavy-based saucepans. Add 150 g/5½ oz blueberries to the first pan and 150 g/5½ oz raspberries to the second. Gently heat both pans for 3–5 minutes, stirring, until the fruit has softened and the sauce thickened. Leave to cool, then stir.

5. When ready to serve, put a teaspoonful of crème fraîche on two-thirds of the biscuits, top half of these with a teaspoon of raspberry compote (you may need to break up the raspberries first), press a cream-topped biscuit on top, then add a teaspoonful of blueberry compote. Complete with a third biscuit, then transfer to a serving plate. Top half the stacks with a raspberry and half with a blueberry and dust with sifted icing sugar.

Mini clementine granitas

Makes: 10
Prep: 25 minutes
Cook: 5 minutes
Freeze: 4 hours plus overnight

If you are serving these only to adults you might like to add a splash of Cointreau or Grand Marnier to the mixture before freezing.

10 clementines

85 g/3 oz granulated sugar

4 tbsp water

finely grated rind and juice of
1 lemon

juice of 1 large orange

1. Cut a thin slice off the top of each clementine and set aside. Squeeze a little of the juice from each fruit into a blender. Using a teaspoon, scoop the flesh into the blender, then whizz to a purée.

2. Press the purée through a sieve into a large loaf tin. Put the 10 clementine cups into a roasting tin and freeze.

3. Put the sugar and water into a heavy-based saucepan. Heat gently for 5 minutes, or until the sugar has dissolved, tilting the pan to mix them together. Increase the heat and boil rapidly without stirring for 1 minute. Remove from the heat, then stir in the lemon rind and juice. Pour the lemon syrup and orange juice onto the clementine purée through a sieve and stir, then leave to cool.

4. Transfer the loaf tin to the freezer and freeze for 2 hours, or until the mixture is semi-frozen. Break up the ice crystals using a fork, then return to the freezer for 1 hour. Beat again with the fork, then freeze for 1 more hour. Beat again until it resembles coloured snow.

5. Spoon the granita into the clementine cups, add the lids at a jaunty angle and freeze overnight. (If the granita has frozen too firmly, allow it to soften at room temperature for a few minutes, then beat with a fork.) When ready to serve, transfer the iced desserts to a plate.

Striped cranberry and amaretti creams

Makes: 10
Prep: 30 minutes
Cook: 5-8 minutes
Chill: 1 hour

An easy festive dessert that makes a great alternative to the traditional Christmas pudding. Children will love to help you make the sugar stars.

85 g/3oz caster sugar

2 tsp cornflour

a large pinch of ground cinnamon

a large pinch of ground ginger

125 ml/4 fl oz water

200 g/7 oz frozen cranberries

AMARETTI CREAM

150 g/5½ oz full-fat soft cheese

3 tbsp caster sugar

200 ml/7 fl oz double cream

4 tsp orange juice or Cointreau

55 g/2 oz amaretti biscuits, crushed

SUGAR STARS

icing sugar, for dusting

150 g/5½ oz ready-to-roll fondant icing

1. Put the sugar, cornflour, cinnamon and ginger into a medium heavy-based saucepan, then gradually mix in the water until smooth. Add the frozen cranberries and cook gently for 5–8 minutes, stirring from time to time, until they are soft and the compote has thickened. Cover and leave to cool.

2. For the amaretti cream, put the soft cheese and sugar into a mixing bowl and stir, then gradually whisk in the cream until smooth. Stir in the orange juice and then the biscuit crumbs. Spoon the mixture into a paper or plastic disposable piping bag. Spoon the cranberry compote into another disposable piping bag. Snip off the tips.

3. Pipe the amaretti cream into 10 shot glasses until they are one-quarter full. Pipe over half the cranberry compote, then repeat the layers. Cover and chill in the fridge for 1 hour.

4. For the sugar stars, line a baking tray with non-stick baking paper. Lightly dust a work surface with icing sugar. Knead the icing lightly, then roll it out thinly. Stamp out stars of different sizes using tiny star cutters, then transfer to the prepared baking tray and leave to harden at room temperature for 1 hour, or until needed. Arrange the stars on the desserts and around the bases of the glasses just before you serve them.

Chocolate and caramel cups

Makes: 12
Prep: 30 minutes
Cook: 7–8 minutes
Chill: 2 hours

If you don't have any petit four cases, line the sections of a mini muffin tin with small squares of cling film, spread melted chocolate over the cling film, then peel it away before serving.

150 g/5½ oz plain chocolate, roughly chopped

115 g/4 oz granulated sugar

4 tbsp water

12 small walnut halves

25 g/1 oz unsalted butter

125 ml/4 fl oz double cream

1. Line a 12-section mini muffin tin with paper petit four cases. Line a baking tray with non-stick baking paper.

2. Put the chocolate in a heatproof bowl, set the bowl over a saucepan of gently simmering water and heat until melted. Put a spoonful of melted chocolate into each paper case, then brush over the sides evenly using a small pastry brush. Chill for 30 minutes, then brush on a second layer of chocolate, taking care over the sides so there is an even thickness. Cover and chill in the fridge.

3. Put the sugar and water into a small heavy-based saucepan. Heat gently for 5 minutes, or until the sugar has dissolved, tilting the pan to mix them together. Increase the heat and boil rapidly without stirring for 4–5 minutes, until the caramel is deep golden (see page 7). Remove from the heat, add the walnuts, quickly coat them in the caramel, then lift them out using 2 forks. Put them on the prepared baking tray, slightly apart.

4. Add the butter to the remaining caramel, tilt the pan to mix, then gradually stir in the cream. Transfer to a bowl, leave to cool, then cover and chill in the fridge for 1½ hours, or until thick. Lift the chocolate-lined paper cases out of the tin. Spoon the caramel cream into a large piping bag fitted with a large star nozzle and pipe it into the chocolate cups. Chill in the fridge until required. Decorate with the caramel walnuts just before serving.

1

Mini Party Desserts

Cherry and honey terrines

Makes: 30
Prep: 25 minutes
Cook: 10 minutes
Freeze: 30 minutes
Chill: 5 hours

This two-tone dessert is made by setting the jelly mould at an angle before adding the creamy layer for an eye-catching effect.

300 g/10½ oz frozen stoned cherries

2 tbsp caster sugar

175 ml/6 fl oz water

4 tsp powdered gelatine

250 g/9 oz fromage frais

finely grated rind of 1 lemon

3 tbsp runny honey

150 ml/5 fl oz double cream

1. Put the frozen cherries, sugar and 125 ml/4 fl oz water into a medium heavy-based saucepan, bring to the boil, then reduce the heat and simmer, uncovered, for 5 minutes, until the cherries have softened.

2. Meanwhile, put the remaining water in a small heatproof bowl, then sprinkle the gelatine over the surface, making sure the powder is absorbed. Set aside for 5 minutes. Set the bowl of gelatine in a heavy-based saucepan of gently simmering water and heat for 5 minutes, stirring from time to time, until the gelatine is a clear liquid (see page 7).

3. Whizz the cherry mixture in a blender until puréed, then pour back into the heavy-based saucepan. Stir in 2½ tablespoons of the gelatine mixture, then leave to cool.

4. Divide the cherry mixture between 6 x 150-ml/5-fl oz loaf tins, prop them up in the freezer so that the jelly sets at an angle, then freeze for 30 minutes, or until firm.

5. Meanwhile, put the fromage frais, lemon rind and honey into a mixing bowl and stir together. Pour the cream into a large mixing bowl and whisk until it forms soft swirls, then fold it into the fromage frais mixture. Add the remaining gelatine mixture and stir gently, then cover and leave at room temperature.

6. When the semi-frozen jellies are ready, spoon the fromage frais over the top, level, then cover and chill in the fridge for 4 hours, or until set.

7. To turn out, dip each mould in a dish of just-boiled water for 2 seconds, then lift it out of the water. Loosen the edges of each dessert with a round-bladed knife, then turn out onto a plate, remove the tin and clean up the edge of the jelly with a sharp knife if needed. Return to the fridge for 1 hour, then slice each terrine into 5 and serve.

Honey and pistachio ice cream with poached figs

Makes: 10
Prep: 30–35 minutes
Cook: 10 minutes
Freeze: 1–7 hours

Refreshingly cool and summery, this Greek-inspired dessert can be made in advance and looks best served with small figs.

ICE CREAM

6 egg yolks

2 tsp cornflour

6 tbsp runny honey

450 ml/16 fl oz milk

250 g/9 oz Greek yogurt

2 tsp rosewater (optional)

55 g/2 oz pistachio nuts, roughly chopped

POACHED FIGS

150 ml/5 fl oz red wine

55 g/2 oz caster sugar

1 cinnamon stick, halved

10 small figs

1. For the ice cream, put the egg yolks, cornflour and honey into a large mixing bowl. Put the milk into a medium heavy-based saucepan, bring to the boil, then gradually whisk it into the yolks. Strain the mixture through a sieve back into the pan and cook over a low heat, stirring, until thickened and smooth. Pour the custard into a clean bowl, cover the surface with baking paper and leave to cool.

2. Whisk the yogurt and rosewater, if using, into the custard. Pour the mixture into a chilled ice cream machine and churn for 15–20 minutes, until thick and creamy. Mix in the pistachio nuts and churn until stiff enough to scoop. If you don't have an ice cream machine, pour into a large non-stick loaf tin for 3–4 hours, until semi-frozen. Beat in a food processor, then stir in the pistachio nuts, return to the loaf tin and freeze for a further 3 hours, or until firm.

3. Meanwhile, for the poached figs, put the wine, sugar and cinnamon stick into a small heavy-based saucepan and heat gently. Add the figs (they should fit snugly into the pan) and poach gently for 5 minutes. Leave to cool.

4. When ready to serve, take the ice cream out of the freezer and allow it to soften at room temperature for 5–10 minutes. Scoop into small dishes and add 2 fig halves and a little of the syrup. Serve immediately.

Spiced plum spirals

Makes: 32
Prep: 30 minutes
Cook: 12–15 minutes

There's no need to make your own pastry for these. Simply unroll ready-rolled puff pastry, sprinkle with spiced sugar and orange, then roll up, slice and bake. For this recipe they are sandwiched with a spiced plum filling.

a little sunflower oil, for greasing

100 g/3½ oz caster sugar

1 tsp ground cinnamon

finely grated rind of 1 orange

640 g pack of 2 ready-rolled puff pastry sheets

milk, for brushing

FILLING

300 g/10½ oz plums, stoned and finely chopped

40 g/1½ oz caster sugar

a large pinch of ground cinnamon

3 tbsp water

1 tsp cornflour

icing sugar, sifted, for dusting

1. Preheat the oven to 200°C/400°F/Gas Mark 6. Lightly brush 2 baking trays with oil.

2. Put the sugar, cinnamon and orange rind into a mixing bowl and stir.

3. Unroll a pastry sheet, roll it out if necessary, then cut it in half to make 2 x 23 x 19-cm/9 x 7½-inch pieces. Sprinkle both pieces with half the sugar mixture, then roll them up, starting with a long edge, and brush a little milk onto the ends to stick them in place. Cut each roll into 16 slices, then put the slices, cut-side-up, on one of the prepared baking trays.

4. Repeat step 3 with the second pastry sheet. Bake in the preheated oven for 12–15 minutes, until golden.

5. Meanwhile, for the filling, put the plums into a heavy-based saucepan and add the sugar, cinnamon and 2 tablespoons of water. Cover with a lid and cook over a gentle heat for 10 minutes. Mix the cornflour with the remaining 1 tablespoon of water in a small bowl, then stir it into the plums and cook for 1 minute more, until thickened. Leave to cool.

6. Put a spoonful of the plum filling onto half the pastries, then top each with another pastry. Arrange on a serving plate and lightly dust with icing sugar.

Blueberry vodka jellies

Makes: 12
Prep: 15 minutes
Cook: 8 minutes
Chill: 4 hours

This pretty dessert can be prepared in minutes. It looks stylish served in glasses of different heights then arranged on individual dessert plates or saucers and scattered with pink edible glitter.

6 trifle sponges or thin slices of shop-bought Madeira cake

350 ml/12 fl oz water

3 tsp powdered gelatine

250 g/9 oz blueberries

70 g/2½ oz caster sugar

finely grated rind of 1 lemon

100 ml/3½ fl oz vodka

125 ml/4 fl oz double cream

pink edible glitter, to decorate

1. Cut out 12 small circles of sponge, using the top of a liqueur glass as a guide, then press each of them into the base of a liqueur glass.

2. Put 50 ml/2 fl oz water into a small bowl, then sprinkle the gelatine over the surface, making sure the powder is absorbed. Set aside for 5 minutes.

3. Meanwhile, put the blueberries, sugar, lemon rind and remaining 300 ml/10 fl oz water into a heavy-based saucepan and bring to the boil, then reduce the heat and simmer, uncovered, for 5 minutes, until the fruit has softened.

4. Take the pan off the heat, add the gelatine and stir until it has dissolved. Add the vodka, then pour the mixture into the glasses, pressing down the sponge circles with a teaspoon if they begin to float. Leave to cool, then cover and put the glasses on a small baking tray. Chill in the fridge for 4 hours, or until set.

5. When ready to serve, spoon 2 teaspoons of the cream over the top of each dessert, then sprinkle with pink edible glitter.

Iced chocolate and peppermint mousses

Makes: 12
Prep: 40 minutes
Cook: 10 minutes
Freeze: 4 hours

A classic French dessert with a twist. As these little mousses are frozen, they can be made well in advance of your party. The drizzled chocolate decoration can be prepared the night before and left in the fridge until you are ready to serve.

150 g/5½ oz plain chocolate, roughly chopped

15 g/½ oz unsalted butter, diced

3 eggs, separated

2 tbsp milk

1 tbsp caster sugar

½ tsp peppermint extract

DECORATION

55 g/2 oz plain chocolate, roughly chopped

55 g/2 oz white chocolate, roughly chopped

a few drops of green food colouring

125 ml/4 fl oz double cream

½–1 tsp peppermint extract

1. For the mousse, put the plain chocolate and butter in a heatproof bowl, set the bowl over a saucepan of gently simmering water and heat until melted. Stir in the egg yolks, one at a time, then stir in the milk until smooth. Remove from the heat.

2. Whisk the egg whites in a large, clean mixing bowl until you have soft peaks. Gradually whisk in the sugar a teaspoonful at a time. Fold the egg whites into the melted chocolate mixture, then fold in the peppermint.

3. Spoon the mousse into 12 plastic shot glasses (if you have a funnel or large piping nozzle, spoon the mousse into this and pipe it into the glasses so that the sides don't get messy). Freeze for 4 hours, or overnight.

4. Meanwhile, for the decoration, line a baking tray with non-stick baking paper. Put the plain chocolate in a heatproof bowl, set the bowl over a heavy-based saucepan of gently simmering water and heat until melted. Drizzle spoonfuls of the melted chocolate over the prepared baking tray in random squiggles, then chill in the fridge for 30 minutes.

5. Put the white chocolate for the decoration in a heatproof bowl, set the bowl over a heavy-based saucepan of gently simmering water and heat until melted. Drizzle half the melted white chocolate over the plain chocolate on the baking tray. Stir the green food colouring into the remaining white chocolate and drizzle this over the other 2 layers of chocolate. Chill in the fridge for 30 minutes.

6. To decorate the mousses, pour the cream into a large bowl and whisk until it forms soft swirls, then stir in the peppermint extract. Spoon this onto the frozen desserts, then break the drizzled chocolate into pieces and press it into the cream. Allow the desserts to stand at room temperature for 10 minutes, then serve.

Tropical caramel custards

Makes: 10
Prep: 25 minutes
Cook: 30–35 minutes
Chill: 4 hours

A favourite dessert gets an exotic twist, with the addition of orange, lime and mango. If you don't have small metal pudding moulds, use little foil muffin or tart cases, but make sure they're 4 cm / 1½ inches deep.

175 g/6 oz granulated sugar

175 ml/6 fl oz water

3 tbsp boiling water

2 eggs, plus 2 egg yolks

150 ml/5 fl oz semi-skimmed milk

400 g/14 oz can sweetened full-fat condensed milk

finely grated rind of 1 orange

finely grated rind of 1 lime

½ small mango, peeled and stoned, to decorate

1. Preheat the oven to 160°C/325°F/Gas Mark 3. Put 10 x 150-ml/5-fl oz metal pudding or dariole moulds in a roasting tin.

2. Put the sugar and water into a heavy-based saucepan. Heat gently for 5 minutes, or until the sugar has dissolved, tilting the pan to mix them together. Increase the heat and boil rapidly without stirring for 5 minutes, until the caramel is deep golden (see page 7). Remove from the heat and add the boiling water, but stand well back as the syrup will spit. Allow the syrup to cool for 1 minute, or until the bubbles begin to subside, then divide it between the moulds.

3. Put the eggs and egg yolks into a large jug, then whisk lightly with a fork.

4. Pour the milk and condensed milk into a heavy-based saucepan. Bring just to the boil over a low heat, stirring constantly. Slowly pour this into the egg yolks, then strain back into the pan. Stir in the orange rind and half the lime rind (wrap the rest in cling film and reserve).

5. Pour the custard into the moulds. Pour warm water into the roasting tin to come halfway up the sides of the moulds. Bake in the preheated oven for 20–25 minutes, or until the custard is set. Lift the moulds out of the water, allow to cool, then chill in the fridge for 4 hours, or overnight.

6. To serve, cut the mango into small, thin slices. Dip each mould in a dish of just-boiled water for 10 seconds, then lift it out of the water. Loosen the edges of each dessert with a round-bladed knife, then invert them out onto a plate and remove the mould. Serve topped with the mango slices and sprinkled with the reserved lime rind.

Mini chocolate éclairs with Irish cream

Makes: 36
Prep: 45 minutes
Cook: 20-25 minutes
Set: 15 minutes

A great crowd-pleaser, but if serving to a gathering of mixed ages you may prefer to divide the cream and add just 2 tablespoons of Irish cream liqueur to half the cream, serving the liqueur-free version to the children.

55 g/2 oz unsalted butter, plus extra for greasing

150 ml/5 fl oz water

70 g/2½ oz plain flour

a pinch of salt

2 eggs, beaten

a few drops of vanilla extract

FILLING

350 ml/12 fl oz double cream

2 tbsp icing sugar, sifted

4 tbsp Irish cream liqueur

TOPPING

25 g/1 oz unsalted butter, diced

100 g/3½ oz plain chocolate, roughly chopped

1 tbsp icing sugar, sifted

2 tsp milk

1. Preheat the oven to 200°C/400°F/Gas Mark 6. Lightly grease 2 baking trays with butter.

2. Put the butter and water into a medium heavy-based saucepan and heat gently until the butter has melted. Increase the heat and bring to the boil, then remove from the heat. Sift in the flour and salt, then return the pan to the heat and stir together until the mixture makes a smooth ball that leaves the sides of the pan clean. Leave to cool for at least 15 minutes.

3. Gradually beat in the eggs, beating well after each addition, until the mixture is smooth. Stir in the vanilla. Spoon the mixture into a large piping bag fitted with a 1.5-cm/⅝-inch plain piping nozzle, then pipe 4-cm/1½-inch long éclairs onto the prepared baking trays.

4. Bake in the preheated oven for 10–12 minutes, until well risen and crisp on the outside. Make a slit in the side of each éclair to allow the steam to escape, then put them back in the oven for 2 minutes. Leave to cool.

5. About 1 hour before serving, make the filling. Pour the cream into a large mixing bowl, add the sifted icing sugar and cream liqueur, and whisk until it forms soft swirls. Spoon this into a piping bag fitted with a star tube, then pipe it into the éclairs.

6. For the topping, put all the ingredients in a heatproof bowl, set the bowl over a heavy-based saucepan of gently simmering water and heat until melted, smooth and glossy, stirring once or twice. Spoon this over the éclairs, leave to set for 15 minutes, then transfer to a serving plate.

Coffee parfait bites

Makes: 20
Prep: 30 minutes
Cook: 12–15 minutes
Set: 1½ hours

Bite through the crisp coffee meringue into the creamy, smooth coffee parfait filling. If you serve these in pretty paper cases, you won't need to offer guests plates.

175 g/6 oz icing sugar

85 g/3 oz light muscovado sugar

115 g/4 oz ground almonds

3 large egg whites

100 g/3½ oz plain chocolate, roughly chopped, to decorate

PARFAIT

55 g/2 oz granulated sugar

3 tbsp water

2 egg yolks

2 tsp instant coffee granules

105 g/4 oz unsalted butter, softened and diced

1. Line 3 baking trays with non-stick baking paper. Put the icing sugar, light muscovado sugar and ground almonds into a food processor and whizz until finely ground, then press through a sieve into a mixing bowl and set aside.

2. Whisk the egg whites in a large, clean mixing bowl until you have soft peaks. Gently fold half the sugar-and-almond mixture into the eggs using a large spoon, then fold in the remaining mixture until you have a smooth, soft meringue that falls gently from the spoon.

3. Spoon the mixture into a piping bag fitted with a large, plain nozzle and pipe rounds about 2.5 cm/1 inch in diameter onto the paper, leaving a little space between them. Leave to stand for 10–15 minutes to dry. Preheat the oven to 160°C/325°F/Gas Mark 3.

4. Bake the macaroons in the preheated oven for 12–15 minutes, or until they can be lifted off the paper, then leave to cool.

5. For the parfait, put the granulated sugar and water into a heavy-based saucepan. Heat gently for 4–5 minutes, until the sugar has dissolved, tilting the pan to mix them together. Increase the heat and boil rapidly without stirring until the temperature reaches 115°C/239°F on a sugar thermometer, or until there is a hint of colour around the edges.

6. Meanwhile, put the egg yolks into a mixing bowl, then whisk in the coffee. As soon as the syrup is ready, gradually whisk it into the yolks in a thin trickle until the mixture is thick and cool, then whisk in the butter piece by piece. Cover and leave to cool, then sandwich the macaroons together in pairs with the parfait.

7. For the decoration, put the chocolate in a heatproof bowl, set the bowl over a heavy-based saucepan of gently simmering water and heat until melted. Put the melted chocolate into a paper piping bag and snip off the tip, then pipe zigzag lines over the top of the macaroons. Leave in a cool place for the chocolate to harden, then serve.

Index